The Harlem Renaissance

American history, Volume 22

Michael Johnson

Published by Harmony House Publishing, 2024.

THE HARLEM RENAISSANCE

First edition. April 4, 2024.

Copyright © 2024 Michael Johnson.

ISBN: 979-8224352265

Written by Michael Johnson.

Table of Contents

"To the resilient spirit of the Harlem community, past and present, whose creativity, courage, and resilience ignited a cultural renaissance that continues to inspire generations. This book is dedicated to those who dared to dream, who dared to create, and who dared to challenge the status quo. May their legacy forever illuminate our path toward a more inclusive, equitable, and vibrant world."

Chapter 1: Introduction to the Harlem Renaissance

Setting the Stage: Overview of Harlem in the Early 20th Century

Harlem, a neighborhood in the northern section of Manhattan, New York City, emerged as the epicenter of African American culture and creativity during the early 20th century. Prior to the Harlem Renaissance, Harlem was primarily a white neighborhood, but due to rapid urbanization and migration patterns, its demographics underwent a significant transformation.

In the late 19th and early 20th centuries, millions of African Americans migrated from the rural South to urban centers in the North, seeking better economic opportunities and fleeing the oppressive Jim Crow laws and racial violence. This mass movement, known as the Great Migration, profoundly impacted cities like New York, with Harlem becoming a major destination for Black migrants.

Historical Context: Factors Leading to the Cultural Rebirth

Several interconnected factors contributed to the emergence of the Harlem Renaissance:

1. The Great Migration: The influx of Black migrants from the South brought with it a wealth of talent, creativity, and ambition. These individuals, escaping the constraints of segregation, brought their rich cultural heritage and traditions to Harlem, creating a vibrant and dynamic community.

2. Urbanization and Industrialization: The rapid urbanization and industrialization of American society during the early 20th century created new opportunities for African Americans in cities like New York. While many faced discrimination and economic hardship, others found jobs in factories, businesses, and cultural institutions, enabling them to build new lives and communities in urban centers.

3. Intellectual and Artistic Ferment: The early 20th century witnessed a flowering of intellectual and artistic activity among African Americans, fueled by a desire for self-expression and social change. Black intellectuals, writers, artists, and musicians sought to challenge racial stereotypes, celebrate their cultural heritage, and assert their identity as a people.

4. Political and Social Activism: The Harlem Renaissance was also shaped by the broader social and political currents of the time, including the fight for civil rights and racial equality. Organizations like the NAACP (National Association for the Advancement of Colored People) and the Urban League worked to combat racism and discrimination, while individuals like W.E.B. Du Bois and Marcus Garvey advocated for Black empowerment and self-determination.

5. Cultural Exchange and Collaboration: Harlem's vibrant and diverse community fostered a spirit of collaboration and exchange among artists, writers, musicians, and intellectuals from different backgrounds and disciplines. This cross-pollination of ideas and influences helped to fuel the creative energy of the Harlem Renaissance and produce groundbreaking works of art and literature.

In summary, the Harlem Renaissance was a cultural and intellectual movement that emerged in Harlem during the early 20th century, fueled by the convergence of the Great Migration, urbanization, artistic ferment, political activism, and cultural exchange. It represented a profound expression of African American identity, creativity, and resilience in the face of oppression and adversity, leaving an indelible mark on American culture and society.

Chapter 2: The Great Migration

Exploring the Mass Migration of African Americans to Harlem

The Great Migration, one of the most significant demographic shifts in American history, refers to the mass movement of African Americans from the rural South to urban centers in the North, Midwest, and West between the early 20th century and the 1970s. Harlem, a neighborhood in Manhattan, New York City, emerged as one of the primary destinations for Black migrants during this period. This chapter delves into the causes and consequences of the Great Migration, with a specific focus on its impact on Harlem's cultural landscape and demographics.

Causes of the Great Migration:

1. Escaping Jim Crow: African Americans in the South faced widespread segregation, discrimination, and racial violence under the Jim Crow laws. The promise of freedom from these oppressive conditions motivated many to seek a better life in the North, where they hoped to find greater economic opportunities, social equality, and political freedom.

2. Economic Opportunity: The decline of the agricultural economy in the South, exacerbated by factors such as mechanization, crop failures, and low wages, pushed many Black families to seek employment in Northern industries, such as manufacturing, mining, and steel production. The booming industrial economy of the North promised higher wages, better working conditions, and the possibility of upward mobility.

3. The Pull of the North: The North was perceived as a land of opportunity and promise, where African Americans could escape the limitations and constraints of the segregated South and build new lives for themselves and their families. The vibrant urban centers of the North, with their bustling streets, cultural institutions, and diverse communities, held a particular allure for migrants seeking a fresh start.

4. Push Factors: In addition to the pull of economic opportunity and social freedom, African Americans in the South were also driven to migrate by a desire to escape racial violence, lynchings, and other forms of persecution. The Ku Klux Klan and other white supremacist groups terrorized Black communities, leading many to flee in search of safety and security.

Impact on Harlem's Cultural Landscape and Demographics:

1. Population Growth: The Great Migration transformed the demographic makeup of Harlem, turning it into a predominantly African American neighborhood. Between 1910 and 1930, Harlem's population exploded, growing from around 50,000 to over 200,000 residents, with the majority being Black migrants from the South. This influx of new arrivals reshaped the social fabric of Harlem, creating a vibrant and dynamic community.

2. Cultural Diversity: The Great Migration brought together African Americans from different regions, backgrounds, and cultural traditions, creating a rich tapestry of diversity within Harlem. Southern migrants brought with them their own customs, dialects, music, and cuisine, contributing to the cultural mosaic of the neighborhood. Harlem became a melting pot of Black culture, where

people from all walks of life came together to celebrate their shared heritage and identity.

3. Artistic and Intellectual Flourishing: The influx of Black migrants to Harlem fueled a creative renaissance, giving rise to a flourishing of art, literature, music, and intellectual discourse known as the Harlem Renaissance. Writers, artists, musicians, and intellectuals flocked to Harlem, drawn by the energy, excitement, and sense of possibility that permeated the neighborhood. The Harlem Renaissance produced some of the most iconic and enduring works of African American culture, including the poetry of Langston Hughes, the novels of Zora Neale Hurston, and the music of Duke Ellington.

4. Economic Development: The Great Migration stimulated economic growth and development in Harlem, as new businesses, restaurants, nightclubs, and cultural institutions sprang up to serve the needs and desires of the burgeoning Black community. Harlem became a center of Black entrepreneurship and commerce, with businesses owned and operated by African Americans catering to the tastes and preferences of their fellow residents. The economic vitality of Harlem attracted investment and attention from outside investors, further fueling its growth and development.

5. Social and Political Activism: The Great Migration also had profound implications for the struggle for civil rights and social justice in America. Harlem became a hotbed of activism and organizing, as African Americans mobilized to challenge racial discrimination, segregation, and inequality. Organizations like the NAACP, the Urban League, and the Marcus Garvey's Universal Negro Improvement Association (UNIA) found a receptive audience in Harlem, where residents were eager to fight for their rights and demand equality under the law.

In summary, the Great Migration transformed Harlem into a vibrant and dynamic hub of African American culture, creativity, and activism. The influx of Black migrants from the South reshaped the neighborhood's demographic makeup, cultural landscape, and social fabric, laying the groundwork for the Harlem Renaissance and the emergence of a new era of Black pride, identity, and empowerment.

Chapter 3: Pre-Harlem Renaissance Cultural Landscape

Brief Overview of African American Culture before the Renaissance

The period preceding the Harlem Renaissance was characterized by significant challenges and struggles for African Americans, yet it was also a time of cultural resilience, creativity, and resistance. This chapter provides an overview of African American culture before the Harlem Renaissance, highlighting key figures and movements that laid the groundwork for the cultural rebirth that would follow.

1. Slavery and Resistance:

African American culture has deep roots in the experience of slavery, which profoundly shaped the identity, traditions, and artistic expressions of Black people in America. Despite the brutal conditions of enslavement, African Americans maintained their cultural heritage through music, storytelling, religion, and communal traditions. Spirituals, work songs, and folk tales served as expressions of resistance, resilience, and solidarity among enslaved communities.

2. Reconstruction and Jim Crow:

Following the abolition of slavery, African Americans faced new challenges during the Reconstruction era and the subsequent rise of Jim Crow segregation. Despite the promise of freedom and citizenship, Black people continued to confront systemic racism, violence, and disenfranchisement in the South. However, during this period, there were also significant strides in education, political representation, and cultural expression, as Black communities worked to build institutions and create spaces for self-determination.

3. The Rise of Black Institutions:

Throughout the late 19th and early 20th centuries, African Americans established a network of institutions to support their communities and advance their interests. Historically Black colleges and universities (HBCUs) emerged as centers of learning and scholarship, producing generations of leaders, intellectuals, and activists. Churches, fraternal organizations, and mutual aid societies provided social, economic, and spiritual support to Black communities, fostering a sense of solidarity and collective identity.

4. Literary and Intellectual Traditions:

African American literature and intellectual thought flourished in the late 19th and early 20th centuries, laying the foundation for the literary renaissance of the Harlem Renaissance. Writers such as Frederick Douglass, Harriet Jacobs, and Booker T. Washington challenged racist stereotypes and advocated for the rights and dignity of Black people through their autobiographies, essays, and speeches. The works of W.E.B. Du Bois, Ida B. Wells, and Anna Julia Cooper contributed to the development of Black intellectual thought and the articulation of a distinct African American cultural identity.

5. Artistic and Musical Innovations:

African American artists and musicians made significant contributions to American culture long before the Harlem Renaissance. Visual artists like Henry Ossawa Tanner and Edmonia Lewis achieved international recognition for their portrayals of Black life and history, challenging prevailing notions of race and beauty. In music, genres such as ragtime, blues, and jazz emerged from the fusion of African and European musical traditions, providing a soundtrack for Black life and expression.

6. Social and Political Activism:

Throughout the late 19th and early 20th centuries, African Americans organized and mobilized to challenge racial discrimination, segregation, and violence. Civil rights organizations such as the NAACP, founded in 1909, advocated for legal and political equality through litigation, lobbying, and public education campaigns. Grassroots movements such as Marcus Garvey's Universal Negro Improvement Association (UNIA) promoted Black pride, self-reliance, and economic empowerment, laying the groundwork for the Black nationalist and Pan-Africanist movements of the Harlem Renaissance era.

Highlighting Key Figures and Movements Laying the Groundwork for the Renaissance

1. Booker T. Washington:

Booker T. Washington was one of the most influential African American leaders of the late 19th and early 20th centuries. As the founder of the Tuskegee Institute in Alabama, Washington emphasized vocational education and economic self-sufficiency as the path to Black advancement. His autobiography, "Up from Slavery," became a bestseller and a powerful testament to the resilience and determination of African Americans in the face of adversity.

2. W.E.B. Du Bois:

W.E.B. Du Bois was a pioneering sociologist, historian, and civil rights activist who played a central role in shaping African American intellectual thought and political activism. Du Bois's seminal work,

"The Souls of Black Folk," explored the double consciousness of African Americans, grappling with the conflict between their African heritage and their American citizenship. As a co-founder of the NAACP and editor of its magazine, "The Crisis," Du Bois advocated for racial equality, social justice, and cultural pride.

3. Ida B. Wells:

Ida B. Wells was a fearless journalist, suffragist, and anti-lynching crusader who exposed the horrors of racial violence and discrimination in the South. Through her investigative reporting and activism, Wells challenged the prevailing narratives of white supremacy and advocated for the rights and dignity of Black people. Her work laid the groundwork for the civil rights movement and inspired generations of activists to fight for racial justice.

4. Paul Laurence Dunbar:

Paul Laurence Dunbar was one of the first African American poets to achieve national acclaim for his literary work. Dunbar's poetry, written in both standard English and African American dialect, captured the richness and complexity of Black life in America. His collections, including "Lyrics of Lowly Life" and "Lyrics of the Hearthside," explored themes of love, longing, and resilience, earning him recognition as the "poet laureate of the Negro race."

5. The New Negro Movement:

The New Negro Movement, also known as the Harlem Renaissance, was a cultural and intellectual movement that emerged in the early 20th century, laying the groundwork for the cultural rebirth that would follow. Led by a new generation of African American artists, writers, musicians, and intellectuals, the New Negro Movement sought to challenge racial stereotypes, celebrate Black culture, and assert the dignity and humanity of Black people.

Through literature, art, music, and activism, the New Negro Movement paved the way for a new era of cultural pride, creativity, and resistance in America.

In summary, the period preceding the Harlem Renaissance was marked by significant achievements, struggles, and innovations in African American culture. Despite the challenges of slavery, segregation, and discrimination, Black people forged a vibrant and resilient cultural heritage that laid the groundwork for the cultural renaissance of the Harlem Renaissance. Key figures and movements such as Booker T. Washington, W.E.B. Du Bois, Ida B. Wells, Paul Laurence Dunbar, and the New Negro Movement played crucial roles in shaping African American identity, thought, and expression, paving the way for the artistic and intellectual flowering that would follow.

Chapter 4: Harlem Renaissance: Origins and Influences

Examining the Intellectual, Social, and Artistic Influences Leading to the Renaissance

The Harlem Renaissance was a cultural and intellectual movement that emerged in the 1920s and 1930s, centered in the Harlem neighborhood of New York City. This chapter explores the origins and influences that paved the way for the Harlem Renaissance, examining the intellectual, social, and artistic currents that converged to create a fertile ground for creative expression and cultural rebirth.

1. The Intellectual Climate:

The early 20th century witnessed a flowering of intellectual and artistic activity among African Americans, fueled by a desire for self-expression, social change, and racial pride. Influential thinkers such as W.E.B. Du Bois, Alain Locke, and James Weldon Johnson articulated new visions of Black identity, culture, and politics, laying the groundwork for the Harlem Renaissance. Du Bois's concept of "double consciousness," Locke's notion of the "New Negro," and Johnson's advocacy for cultural nationalism provided intellectual frameworks that shaped the artistic and cultural expressions of the era.

2. Social and Cultural Transformations:

The post-World War I era brought significant social and cultural transformations to American society, setting the stage for the Harlem Renaissance. The Great Migration, which saw millions of

African Americans migrate from the rural South to urban centers in the North, Midwest, and West, created new opportunities for cultural exchange and collaboration. The proliferation of urban nightlife, the rise of mass media and advertising, and the emergence of new technologies such as radio and phonograph records provided platforms for the dissemination of African American culture to a wider audience.

3. Artistic Innovations:

The Harlem Renaissance was characterized by a flourishing of artistic innovation across multiple disciplines, including literature, visual arts, music, theater, and dance. Writers such as Langston Hughes, Zora Neale Hurston, Claude McKay, and Jean Toomer explored themes of Black identity, heritage, and experience in their poetry, fiction, and essays, challenging racial stereotypes and celebrating the richness and complexity of Black life. Visual artists like Aaron Douglas, Romare Bearden, and Jacob Lawrence used their art to depict the vibrancy and vitality of Harlem's Black community, while musicians like Duke Ellington, Louis Armstrong, and Bessie Smith revolutionized American music with their innovative styles and compositions.

4. Cultural Exchange and Collaboration:

Harlem's vibrant and diverse community fostered a spirit of collaboration and exchange among artists, writers, musicians, and intellectuals from different backgrounds and disciplines. Cultural institutions such as the Harlem YMCA, the Harlem Branch of the New York Public Library, and the Harlem Community Art Center provided spaces for artistic and intellectual engagement, hosting lectures, exhibitions, performances, and discussions that brought together Black and white audiences alike. Literary salons, jazz clubs, and social gatherings provided opportunities for creative networking and cross-pollination of ideas, fueling the creative energy of the Harlem Renaissance.

Role of World War I and Post-War Disillusionment

World War I had a profound impact on American society and culture, contributing to the disillusionment and upheaval that laid the groundwork for the Harlem Renaissance. The war brought about significant social and economic changes, disrupting traditional social hierarchies and challenging prevailing notions of race, nationality, and identity. African American soldiers served with distinction in the war, fighting for democracy and freedom abroad while facing discrimination and segregation at home.

The experience of African American soldiers during World War I contributed to a growing sense of racial consciousness and militancy among Black communities, as they returned home from the war determined to assert their rights and demand equality. The war also led to the Great Migration, as African Americans migrated from the rural South to urban centers in the North, seeking economic opportunities and fleeing the violence and oppression of Jim Crow segregation.

The post-war period was characterized by a sense of disillusionment and alienation among many Americans, as the ideals of progress, democracy, and modernity were called into question in the wake of the war's devastation and disillusionment. African Americans, who had fought and sacrificed for their country, returned home to find themselves still subjected to racism, discrimination, and violence.

In this context, Harlem emerged as a symbol of hope and possibility for African Americans seeking to build new lives and communities in the North. The cultural vitality and creativity of Harlem's Black community provided a beacon of inspiration for artists, writers, musicians, and intellectuals seeking to make sense of the complexities of post-war America and to articulate new visions of Black identity, culture, and politics.

In summary, the Harlem Renaissance was a product of multiple influences and currents, including the intellectual climate of the early 20th century, the social and cultural transformations of the post-World War I era, and the artistic innovations of African American artists, writers, musicians, and intellectuals. World War I and the disillusionment of the post-war period played a significant role in shaping the cultural and intellectual ferment that led to the Harlem Renaissance, providing both inspiration and impetus for African Americans to assert their voice and agency in American society.

Chapter 5: Literary Giants of the Renaissance

Profiles of Influential Writers: Langston Hughes, Zora Neale Hurston, and Claude McKay

1. Langston Hughes:

Langston Hughes (1902-1967) was one of the most prominent and prolific writers of the Harlem Renaissance. Born in Joplin, Missouri, Hughes moved to Harlem in the early 1920s, where he became a central figure in the literary and cultural scene of the neighborhood. Known for his innovative use of language, rhythm, and vernacular speech, Hughes captured the spirit and struggles of African American life in his poetry, fiction, essays, and plays.

Hughes's poetry, characterized by its simplicity, authenticity, and emotional resonance, explored themes of racial pride, identity, and social justice. His most famous poem, "The Negro Speaks of Rivers," written at the age of 17, reflects Hughes's deep connection to the African American experience and heritage. Other notable works include "The Weary Blues," "Montage of a Dream Deferred," and "Harlem," which famously asks, "What happens to a dream deferred?"

In addition to his poetry, Hughes wrote extensively in other genres, including fiction, drama, and autobiography. His novels, such as "Not Without Laughter" and "Simple Speaks His Mind," depict the lives of ordinary Black people with compassion, humor, and insight. Hughes's essays and articles addressed issues of race, politics, and culture, advocating for social and economic equality for African Americans.

2. Zora Neale Hurston:

Zora Neale Hurston (1891-1960) was a pioneering novelist, folklorist, and anthropologist whose work played a central role in the development of African American literature and cultural studies. Born in Alabama and raised in Eatonville, Florida, the first incorporated Black town in the United States, Hurston drew upon her experiences growing up in the rural South to create vivid and authentic portrayals of Black life and culture.

Hurston's most famous novel, "Their Eyes Were Watching God," published in 1937, is considered a masterpiece of American literature. The novel follows the journey of Janie Crawford, a Black woman in search of love, independence, and self-discovery in the rural South. Through Janie's story, Hurston explores themes of race, gender, and identity with lyrical prose and profound insight.

In addition to her fiction, Hurston was also a pioneering anthropologist and folklorist, conducting groundbreaking research on African American folklore, religion, and culture. Her collection of folklore, "Mules and Men," and her study of Haitian voodoo, "Tell My Horse," remain influential works in the field of cultural anthropology.

Hurston's work fell out of favor in the years following her death but experienced a revival in the late 20th century, thanks to the efforts of scholars and writers who recognized her contributions to African American literature and culture.

3. Claude McKay:

Claude McKay (1889-1948) was a Jamaican-born poet, novelist, and essayist whose work played a crucial role in the development of African American literature and political thought. McKay's early poetry, collected in works such as "Songs of Jamaica" and "Constab Ballads," celebrated the beauty and resilience of the Jamaican people while also addressing themes of colonialism, racism, and oppression.

McKay's move to the United States in 1912 exposed him to the harsh realities of racism and discrimination, inspiring him to become an outspoken advocate for Black liberation and social justice. His poem "If We Must Die," written in response to the wave of racial violence and lynchings that swept the country in the aftermath of World War I, became a rallying cry for African Americans and oppressed peoples around the world.

McKay's most famous novel, "Home to Harlem," published in 1928, is considered one of the first major works of African American literature to portray the lives of working-class Black people with honesty and authenticity. The novel follows the experiences of Jake, a Black soldier returning home from World War I, as he navigates the streets of Harlem and grapples with questions of identity, belonging, and social change.

In addition to his fiction, McKay wrote extensively on politics, culture, and race, advocating for Black self-determination and international solidarity. His essays, collected in works such as "Harlem: Negro Metropolis" and "A Long Way from Home," offer incisive critiques of racism, capitalism, and imperialism, and articulate a vision of a world free from oppression and exploitation.

Analysis of Their Works and Contributions to African American Literature

Langston Hughes, Zora Neale Hurston, and Claude McKay were instrumental in shaping the literary landscape of the Harlem

Renaissance and beyond, each making unique contributions to African American literature and culture.

1. Langston Hughes:

Langston Hughes's poetry is characterized by its accessibility, authenticity, and universality. Drawing upon the rhythms and idioms of African American speech and music, Hughes's poetry captures the joys, sorrows, hopes, and dreams of ordinary Black people with lyrical simplicity and emotional depth. His use of the blues and jazz as literary forms revolutionized American poetry, paving the way for generations of poets to come.

Hughes's commitment to portraying the everyday experiences of African Americans with honesty and dignity made him a beloved figure in the Black community and a powerful voice for social change. His works addressed issues of race, class, and identity in America, challenging stereotypes and advocating for the rights and humanity of Black people. Hughes's influence extended beyond literature to music, theater, and politics, where his poetry inspired generations of activists and artists to fight for justice and equality.

2. Zora Neale Hurston:

Zora Neale Hurston's novels, short stories, and folklore collections are celebrated for their rich language, vivid characters, and authentic portrayal of African American life and culture. Hurston's use of dialect and vernacular speech, drawn from her experiences growing up in the rural South, brought a sense of immediacy and intimacy to her writing, allowing readers to enter into the world of her characters and experience their joys and sorrows firsthand.

Hurston's exploration of themes such as race, gender, and identity in her fiction challenged prevailing notions of Blackness and womanhood, offering complex and nuanced portrayals of African

American life that defied stereotypes and caricatures. Her commitment to depicting the diversity and complexity of Black experiences, from the rural South to the urban North, made her a pioneering voice in African American literature and a champion of cultural authenticity and self-expression.

Hurston's contributions to African American literature extend beyond her fiction to her work as an anthropologist and folklorist, where she conducted groundbreaking research on African American folklore, religion, and culture. Her collections of folklore and her studies of voodoo and other African-derived religions remain essential texts for scholars and students of African American studies, offering insights into the richness and diversity of Black cultural traditions.

3. Claude McKay:

Claude McKay's poetry and fiction are characterized by their passionate advocacy for Black liberation and social justice. Drawing upon his experiences as a Jamaican immigrant and a Black man living in America, McKay's works address themes of race, identity, and resistance with urgency and intensity. His poetry, infused with the rhythms and cadences of Jamaican patois, captures the beauty and pain of Black life with searing honesty and raw emotion.

McKay's exploration of Black masculinity, sexuality, and political consciousness in his novels and essays challenged prevailing notions of Blackness and masculinity, offering complex and nuanced portrayals of African American identity that defied stereotypes and conventions. His commitment to social and political activism, both in his writing and in his organizing work, made him a leading voice in the struggle for Black liberation and human rights.

McKay's influence extended beyond literature to politics and activism, where his essays and speeches inspired generations of activists and intellectuals to fight for racial and economic justice. His vision of a world free from oppression and exploitation continues to inspire and guide movements for social change around the world.

In summary, Langston Hughes, Zora Neale Hurston, and Claude McKay were literary giants whose works and contributions shaped the literary landscape of the Harlem Renaissance and beyond. Through their poetry, fiction, essays, and activism, they challenged prevailing notions of race, identity, and culture, and advocated for social change, justice, and equality. Their influence continues to be felt in the fields of literature, culture, and politics, inspiring generations of writers, artists, and activists to celebrate the richness and diversity of the African American experience and to fight for a more just and equitable society.

Chapter 6: Artistic Expressions: Visual Arts

Exploration of the Flourishing Visual Arts Scene in Harlem

The Harlem Renaissance was not only a literary and musical movement but also a flourishing period for the visual arts. In the vibrant community of Harlem, African American artists explored themes of identity, race, culture, and social justice through various mediums, including painting, sculpture, photography, and graphic design. This chapter delves into the diverse and dynamic visual arts scene of the Harlem Renaissance, highlighting the works and contributions of prominent artists such as Aaron Douglas and Romare Bearden.

1. The Harlem Community Art Center:

At the heart of the visual arts scene in Harlem was the Harlem Community Art Center, established in 1937 under the auspices of the Works Progress Administration (WPA). The Art Center provided a space for artists to create, exhibit, and teach, offering classes in painting, drawing, sculpture, printmaking, and photography to community members of all ages. The Art Center played a crucial role in nurturing and supporting emerging talent, providing resources, materials, and mentorship to aspiring artists from diverse backgrounds.

2. The Harlem Artists Guild:

The Harlem Artists Guild was another important institution that promoted the work of African American artists during the Harlem Renaissance. Founded in 1935 by a group of Black artists and intellectuals, including Aaron Douglas, Augusta Savage, and Hale Woodruff, the Guild provided a platform for artists to exhibit their work, exchange ideas, and collaborate on projects that addressed social and political issues facing the Black community. The Guild also organized lectures, workshops, and community outreach programs to engage audiences and promote greater appreciation and understanding of African American art.

3. Themes and Motifs:

African American artists of the Harlem Renaissance drew inspiration from a variety of sources, including African art, jazz music, folklore, and the urban landscape of Harlem itself. Many artists sought to celebrate the beauty and resilience of Black culture, challenging stereotypes and reclaiming their heritage through their art. Common themes and motifs included depictions of Black life and history, spiritual and religious imagery, representations of jazz musicians and dancers, and scenes of everyday life in Harlem.

4. Aaron Douglas:

Aaron Douglas (1899-1979) was one of the leading figures of the Harlem Renaissance and a pioneering artist in the field of African American art. Born in Topeka, Kansas, Douglas moved to New York City in the early 1920s, where he quickly established himself as a central figure in the cultural and intellectual life of Harlem. Douglas's distinctive style, characterized by bold geometric forms, dynamic compositions, and simplified figures, revolutionized African American art and helped to define the visual aesthetic of the Harlem Renaissance.

Douglas's most famous works include his illustrations for books by prominent writers such as Langston Hughes, James Weldon Johnson, and W.E.B. Du Bois, which combined elements of African art, modernism, and social realism to create powerful and evocative images of Black life and struggle. His murals, commissioned for public buildings and institutions throughout the country, celebrated the achievements of African Americans and affirmed their place in American history and culture.

5. Romare Bearden:

Romare Bearden (1911-1988) was another influential artist whose work contributed to the visual richness of the Harlem Renaissance. Born in Charlotte, North Carolina, Bearden moved to Harlem as a young man and became deeply immersed in the cultural and intellectual milieu of the neighborhood. Bearden's art drew upon a wide range of influences, including African art, jazz music, literature, and the modernist avant-garde, to create vibrant and dynamic compositions that captured the energy and diversity of African American life.

Bearden's collages, in particular, are celebrated for their innovative use of found materials, such as photographs, magazine clippings, fabric, and paper, to create layered and textured images that evoke the complexities of Black experience. His series of collages inspired by the music of jazz legends such as Duke Ellington and Louis Armstrong are considered masterpieces of modern art, blending abstraction, realism, and symbolism to create visual symphonies that resonate with rhythm and movement.

6. Legacy and Influence:

The contributions of Aaron Douglas, Romare Bearden, and other African American artists of the Harlem Renaissance continue to resonate in the contemporary art world, inspiring generations of artists to explore themes of race, identity, and culture through their work. Their bold experimentation, innovative techniques, and unwavering commitment to social justice helped to redefine the possibilities of African American art and to challenge prevailing notions of beauty, representation, and power. As we continue to grapple with issues of race, inequality, and social justice in our society, the legacy of the Harlem Renaissance artists reminds us of the enduring power of art to inspire, provoke, and transform the world around us.

Chapter 7: The Sound of the Renaissance: Jazz and Music

Evolution of Jazz and Its Significance in the Harlem Renaissance

The Harlem Renaissance was not only a literary and visual arts movement but also a musical revolution, with jazz at its heart. Jazz, a uniquely American art form born out of the African American experience, played a central role in shaping the cultural landscape of Harlem and defining the spirit of the Renaissance. This chapter explores the evolution of jazz and its significance in the Harlem Renaissance, as well as profiles of jazz legends such as Duke Ellington and Louis Armstrong.

1. Origins of Jazz:

Jazz emerged in the late 19th and early 20th centuries in the African American communities of New Orleans, Louisiana. Drawing upon a rich tapestry of musical traditions, including blues, ragtime, spirituals, work songs, and West African rhythms, jazz musicians created a new form of music characterized by improvisation, syncopation, and expressive freedom. Jazz was both a celebration of Black culture and a reflection of the social and cultural dynamics of American society, blending African and European musical influences to create a distinctly American sound.

2. Spread of Jazz:

In the early decades of the 20th century, jazz spread rapidly across the United States, fueled by the migration of African Americans from the rural South to urban centers in the North, Midwest, and West. Cities such as Chicago, New York, Kansas City, and Los Angeles became hotbeds of jazz innovation, with thriving nightclub scenes, dance halls, and speakeasies where musicians could perform and experiment with new sounds and styles. Jazz became the soundtrack of the Roaring Twenties, capturing the energy, excitement, and optimism of the era.

3. Harlem's Jazz Scene:

Harlem, with its vibrant and diverse community of African American artists, intellectuals, and activists, emerged as one of the epicenters of the jazz world during the Harlem Renaissance. Nightclubs such as the Cotton Club, the Savoy Ballroom, and the Apollo Theater became legendary venues where jazz musicians could showcase their talents and entertain audiences from around the world. Harlem's jazz scene was a melting pot of musical styles and influences, blending elements of blues, ragtime, swing, and bebop to create a dynamic and electrifying sound.

4. Significance of Jazz in the Harlem Renaissance:

Jazz played a crucial role in shaping the cultural and social dynamics of the Harlem Renaissance, providing a soundtrack for the era and a means of expression for African American artists, musicians, and intellectuals. Jazz was more than just music; it was a way of life, a form of self-expression, and a means of resistance against the racial injustices and inequalities of American society. Jazz embodied the spirit of the Harlem Renaissance, with its emphasis on creativity, innovation, and freedom of expression.

5. Profiles of Jazz Legends:

a. Duke Ellington (1899-1974):

Duke Ellington was one of the most influential and innovative jazz musicians of the Harlem Renaissance. Born in Washington, D.C., Ellington moved to New York City in the 1920s, where he quickly rose to prominence as a bandleader, composer, and pianist.

Ellington's orchestra, the Duke Ellington Orchestra, became one of the most celebrated and enduring ensembles in jazz history, known for its distinctive sound, sophisticated arrangements, and virtuosic soloists.

Ellington's contributions to jazz were groundbreaking and far-reaching, pioneering new forms and structures that expanded the possibilities of the genre. His compositions, such as "Mood Indigo," "Sophisticated Lady," and "Take the 'A' Train," are now considered classics of the jazz repertoire, admired for their harmonic richness, melodic inventiveness, and rhythmic complexity. Ellington's ability to blend elements of jazz, classical music, and popular song into a cohesive and distinctive style earned him the nickname "the Duke" and cemented his legacy as one of the greatest jazz musicians of all time.

b. Louis Armstrong (1901-1971):

Louis Armstrong, also known as "Satchmo" or "Pops," was another towering figure in the world of jazz during the Harlem Renaissance. Born in New Orleans, Louisiana, Armstrong began his career as a cornet player in the streets of the Crescent City before moving to Chicago and then New York City, where he became a leading figure in the jazz scene of the 1920s and 1930s.

Armstrong's innovative trumpet playing and gravelly voice made him one of the most distinctive and influential voices in jazz history, revolutionizing the art of improvisation and setting new standards for virtuosity and expression. His recordings with his Hot Five and Hot Seven bands, including "West End Blues," "Potato Head Blues," and "St. Louis Blues," are considered masterpieces of early jazz, showcasing Armstrong's technical prowess, emotional depth, and infectious charisma.

In addition to his musical talents, Armstrong was also a charismatic performer and a beloved entertainer, known for his warm personality, infectious smile, and irrepressible sense of humor. His influence extended beyond the world of jazz to popular music, film, and television, making him one of the most recognizable and beloved figures in American culture.

6. Legacy of Jazz in the Harlem Renaissance:

The legacy of jazz in the Harlem Renaissance continues to resonate in the contemporary music world, inspiring generations of musicians to explore new sounds, techniques, and forms of expression. The Harlem Renaissance not only transformed the cultural landscape of America but also paved the way for the global popularity and influence of jazz as an art form. As we continue to celebrate the achievements and contributions of African American artists, musicians, and intellectuals, the legacy of jazz in the Harlem Renaissance serves as a reminder of the power of music to bring people together, to uplift the human spirit, and to inspire positive social change.

Chapter 8: Theater and Performance

Overview of the Vibrant Theater Scene in Harlem

The Harlem Renaissance was not only a literary and musical movement but also a vibrant period for theater and performance. In the heart of Harlem, theaters, cabarets, and performance spaces flourished, providing platforms for African American playwrights, actors, directors, and performers to showcase their talents and tell their stories. This chapter explores the dynamic theater scene of the Harlem Renaissance, highlighting influential plays and performers of the era.

1. The Apollo Theater:

One of the most iconic venues of the Harlem Renaissance was the Apollo Theater, located on 125th Street in the heart of Harlem. Originally opened in 1914 as Hurtig & Seamon's New Burlesque Theater, the Apollo underwent several transformations before becoming the legendary venue it is today. In the 1920s and 1930s, under the management of Frank Schiffman, the Apollo became a showcase for African American talent, hosting vaudeville shows, musical revues, and theatrical productions that attracted audiences from across New York City and beyond.

The Apollo Theater was known for its amateur night competitions, where aspiring performers could audition for a chance to perform on stage and win cash prizes. Many legendary performers got their start at the Apollo, including Ella Fitzgerald, Billie Holiday, James Brown, and Aretha Franklin. The theater's Amateur Night became a launching pad for African American talent, helping to launch the careers of countless singers, dancers, comedians, and musicians.

2. The Lafayette Theater:

Another important venue for African American theater during the Harlem Renaissance was the Lafayette Theater, located on Seventh Avenue in Harlem. Opened in 1912 as a vaudeville house, the Lafayette was one of the few theaters in New York City that catered to Black audiences and featured Black performers. In the 1920s and 1930s, under the management of John Cort, the Lafayette became a hub for African American theater, hosting productions of plays, musicals, and revues that showcased the talents of Black actors, singers, and dancers.

The Lafayette Theater was known for its groundbreaking productions of plays by African American playwrights, including Langston Hughes, Zora Neale Hurston, and Paul Robeson. The theater's productions often addressed themes of race, identity, and social justice, reflecting the concerns and aspirations of the Black community. The Lafayette Theater played a crucial role in promoting and supporting African American theater during the Harlem Renaissance, providing a platform for Black playwrights, actors, and directors to tell their stories and express their creativity.

3. The Federal Theatre Project:

During the Great Depression of the 1930s, the federal government established the Federal Theatre Project (FTP) as part of the Works Progress Administration (WPA) to provide employment for theater professionals and to bring cultural enrichment to communities across the country. The FTP employed thousands of actors, directors, designers, and technicians, including many African Americans, and produced hundreds of plays, musicals, and revues that reflected the diversity and vitality of American theater.

In Harlem, the FTP sponsored several theater companies and productions that showcased the talents of African American artists and addressed the concerns of the Black community. One of the most notable productions was "The Negro Theatre Unit," which was founded in 1935 under the leadership of Hallie Flanagan and produced plays by African American playwrights such as Langston Hughes, Zora Neale Hurston, and Richard Wright. The FTP's productions were staged in community centers, schools, and theaters throughout Harlem, bringing theater and culture to audiences who might not otherwise have had access to live performances.

4. Influential Plays and Performers:

a. "Porgy and Bess" by George Gershwin, DuBose Heyward, and Ira Gershwin:

"Porgy and Bess" is a groundbreaking opera that premiered in 1935 and quickly became one of the most beloved and enduring works of American musical theater. Based on DuBose Heyward's novel "Porgy" and featuring music by George Gershwin and lyrics by Ira Gershwin, "Porgy and Bess" tells the story of Porgy, a disabled beggar, and Bess, a troubled woman, who find love and redemption in the fictional African American community of Catfish Row in Charleston, South Carolina.

"Porgy and Bess" was revolutionary for its time, featuring an all-Black cast and addressing issues of race, poverty, and community with honesty and compassion. The opera's score, which blends elements of jazz, blues, and spirituals with classical music, is considered one of Gershwin's masterpieces, featuring iconic songs such as "Summertime," "I Got Plenty o' Nuttin'," and "It Ain't Necessarily So." "Porgy and Bess" remains a landmark work in American musical theater, celebrated for its richly drawn characters, stirring music, and timeless themes of love and resilience.

b. Paul Robeson:

Paul Robeson (1898-1976) was a multi-talented performer and activist whose contributions to theater and performance during the Harlem Renaissance were groundbreaking and enduring. Born in Princeton, New Jersey, Robeson rose to fame as a singer, actor, and orator, using his talents to advocate for civil rights, social justice, and international solidarity.

Robeson's performances in plays such as "Emperor Jones" by Eugene O'Neill and "Othello" by William Shakespeare were celebrated for their power, intensity, and emotional depth. Robeson's portrayal of the title role in "Othello," in particular, was hailed as one of the greatest performances in the history of American theater, earning him critical acclaim and international recognition.

In addition to his work as an actor, Robeson was also a gifted singer, known for his powerful bass-baritone voice and his renditions of spirituals, folk songs, and protest anthems. Robeson's recordings of songs such as "Ol' Man River," "Go Down Moses," and "Ballad for Americans" became anthems of the civil rights movement and inspired generations of activists and artists to fight for justice and equality.

c. Shuffle Along:

"Shuffle Along" was a groundbreaking musical comedy that premiered on Broadway in 1921 and became one of the most successful and influential shows of the Harlem Renaissance. Written by Noble Sissle and Eubie Blake, with a book by Flournoy Miller and Aubrey Lyles, "Shuffle Along" was the first Broadway musical to be written, produced, and performed by African Americans.

"Shuffle Along" broke new ground in its portrayal of African American life and culture, featuring a predominantly Black cast and addressing issues of race, identity, and social justice with humor, wit, and style. The show's infectious music, energetic choreography, and irrepressible spirit captivated audiences and critics alike, earning rave reviews and setting box office records.

"Shuffle Along" also launched the careers of several African American performers who would go on to become stars of stage and screen, including Josephine Baker, Florence Mills, and Paul Robeson. The show's success paved the way for future generations of African American artists, playwrights, and producers, helping to establish Harlem as a center of Black culture and creativity.

In summary, the theater scene of the Harlem Renaissance was a vibrant and dynamic world of creativity, innovation, and social engagement. From the legendary stages of the Apollo and the Lafayette to the groundbreaking productions of the Federal Theatre Project, African American playwrights, actors, directors, and performers used theater as a means of expression, empowerment, and resistance, challenging stereotypes and advocating for social change. The plays and performers of the Harlem Renaissance continue to inspire and influence artists and audiences today, reminding us of the enduring power of theater to entertain, enlighten, and uplift the human spirit.

Chapter 9: Political and Social Activism

Examination of the Intersection Between Art and Activism During the Renaissance

The Harlem Renaissance was not only a cultural and artistic movement but also a period of political and social activism. African American artists, writers, musicians, and intellectuals used their creative talents to advocate for civil rights, social justice, and racial equality, challenging the systemic racism and discrimination that pervaded American society. This chapter explores the intersection between art and activism during the Harlem Renaissance, as well as profiles of activists and organizations that played a pivotal role in advocating for change.

1. Art as Activism:

Throughout history, art has been a powerful tool for social change and political activism. Artists have used their creative talents to challenge injustice, raise awareness of pressing issues, and inspire action for positive change. During the Harlem Renaissance, African American artists embraced this tradition of art as activism, using their works to critique racism, celebrate Black culture, and advocate for civil rights.

Visual artists such as Aaron Douglas, Romare Bearden, and Jacob Lawrence created powerful images that depicted the struggles and triumphs of African Americans, confronting stereotypes and challenging prevailing notions of race and identity. Writers such as Langston Hughes, Zora Neale Hurston, and Richard Wright used their poetry, fiction, and essays to address issues of racial injustice, economic inequality, and social marginalization, giving voice to the experiences and aspirations of the Black community.

Musicians such as Duke Ellington, Louis Armstrong, and Billie Holiday used their music to protest against racism and segregation, offering messages of hope, resilience, and solidarity in the face of adversity. The Harlem Renaissance was a testament to the power of art to inspire, provoke, and mobilize people for social change, demonstrating the transformative potential of creativity and imagination in the struggle for justice and equality.

2. Profiles of Activists and Organizations:

a. NAACP (National Association for the Advancement of Colored People):

The NAACP was one of the leading civil rights organizations of the Harlem Renaissance, dedicated to fighting against racial discrimination and segregation in the United States. Founded in 1909 by a group of Black and white activists, including W.E.B. Du Bois, Mary White Ovington, and Moorfield Storey, the NAACP worked tirelessly to challenge Jim Crow laws, lynchings, and other forms of racial violence, and to advocate for political and social equality for African Americans.

During the Harlem Renaissance, the NAACP played a pivotal role in promoting the work of African American artists, writers, and intellectuals, providing platforms for them to showcase their talents and to address issues of race and identity. The organization's magazine, The Crisis, edited by W.E.B. Du Bois, featured articles, essays, poetry, and artwork by leading figures of the Harlem Renaissance, amplifying their voices and advocating for social change.

b. Marcus Garvey and the UNIA (Universal Negro Improvement Association):

Marcus Garvey was a Jamaican-born activist and entrepreneur who founded the Universal Negro Improvement Association (UNIA) in 1914 with the goal of promoting Black pride, self-determination, and economic empowerment. Garvey's message of Black nationalism and Pan-Africanism resonated with millions of African Americans during the Harlem Renaissance, offering a vision of unity, solidarity, and self-reliance in the face of racism and oppression.

The UNIA became one of the largest and most influential Black nationalist organizations of the early 20th century, with chapters and branches throughout the United States, the Caribbean, and Africa. The organization's flagship newspaper, The Negro World, edited by Marcus Garvey, provided a platform for African American writers, journalists, and intellectuals to express their views and advocate for social and political change.

Garvey's call for Black economic empowerment and self-sufficiency inspired generations of African Americans to take pride in their heritage, to support Black-owned businesses, and to work towards building strong and prosperous communities. Although Garvey's vision ultimately fell short of its ambitious goals, his legacy continues to inspire movements for Black liberation and empowerment around the world.

c. The Harlem Renaissance and the Civil Rights Movement:

The Harlem Renaissance laid the groundwork for the modern civil rights movement of the 1950s and 1960s, paving the way for the activism and organizing efforts that would ultimately lead to the dismantling of Jim Crow segregation and the passage of landmark civil rights legislation. The artists, writers, musicians, and intellectuals of the Harlem Renaissance helped to create a climate of awareness, consciousness, and resistance that set the stage for the social and political upheavals of the mid-20th century.

The legacy of the Harlem Renaissance continues to inspire and inform contemporary movements for racial justice and equality, reminding us of the enduring power of art, culture, and activism to shape our collective destiny. As we continue to confront the legacy of racism and inequality in our society, the lessons of the Harlem Renaissance serve as a beacon of hope and inspiration, guiding us towards a future of justice, equality, and freedom for all.

Chapter 10: Harlem Renaissance and Identity

Exploration of How the Renaissance Shaped African American Identity and Consciousness

The Harlem Renaissance was a pivotal moment in African American history, shaping not only the cultural landscape of the time but also the identity and consciousness of Black Americans. This chapter delves into the ways in which the Harlem Renaissance influenced African American identity, discussing themes of race, class, and gender in Renaissance literature and art, and examining the complexities of Black identity during this transformative period.

1. Rediscovery and Reclamation of Heritage:

One of the defining features of the Harlem Renaissance was the rediscovery and reclamation of African American heritage and culture. In the aftermath of slavery and Reconstruction, African Americans faced systematic oppression and marginalization, which resulted in the erasure of their history, culture, and identity. The Harlem Renaissance provided a platform for Black artists, writers, and intellectuals to reclaim their heritage and celebrate the richness and diversity of African American culture.

Literature played a central role in this process of rediscovery and reclamation, with writers such as Langston Hughes, Zora Neale Hurston, and Claude McKay exploring themes of Black identity, history, and culture in their works. Hughes, in particular, championed the idea of "the Negro Renaissance," a cultural awakening that celebrated the achievements and contributions of African Americans to American society and culture.

2. The Double Consciousness of W.E.B. Du Bois:

W.E.B. Du Bois, one of the leading intellectuals of the Harlem Renaissance, articulated the concept of "double consciousness" in his seminal work, "The Souls of Black Folk." Du Bois argued that African Americans lived with a dual identity, caught between their African heritage and their American citizenship, and that this dual identity resulted in a sense of "twoness" or "two-ness" that shaped their experiences and perceptions of the world.

Du Bois's concept of double consciousness resonated deeply with African American writers, artists, and thinkers of the Harlem Renaissance, who grappled with questions of identity, belonging, and self-definition in their works. Writers such as Nella Larsen, in her novel "Passing," and Richard Wright, in his novel "Native Son," explored the psychological and emotional complexities of Black identity in a society that sought to deny their humanity and agency.

3. Race, Class, and Gender in Renaissance Literature and Art:

The Harlem Renaissance was marked by a rich diversity of voices and perspectives, reflecting the complexities of African American identity and experience. Writers and artists of the Renaissance explored themes of race, class, and gender in their works, challenging stereotypes and conventions and offering nuanced and multidimensional portrayals of Black life and culture.

In literature, writers such as Nella Larsen, Jessie Fauset, and Angelina Weld Grimké examined the intersections of race, class, and gender in their novels, short stories, and plays, depicting the lives of Black women and men who struggled against social and economic barriers to achieve their dreams and aspirations. Larsen's novel "Quicksand" and Fauset's novel "Plum Bun," for example, explore the challenges faced by Black women navigating the complexities of race, class, and gender in early 20th-century America.

In art, visual artists such as Aaron Douglas, Archibald Motley, and Augusta Savage explored themes of race, identity, and representation in their paintings, sculptures, and other works. Douglas's murals, with their bold geometric forms and stylized figures, celebrated the achievements and contributions of African Americans to American culture and society, while Motley's vibrant and colorful portraits captured the energy and diversity of Black life in Harlem.

4. The Legacy of the Harlem Renaissance:

The legacy of the Harlem Renaissance continues to resonate in the ongoing struggle for racial justice and equality in America. The Renaissance challenged prevailing notions of race, identity, and culture, and affirmed the dignity, humanity, and resilience of the African American people. The themes and ideas explored by writers, artists, and intellectuals of the Harlem Renaissance laid the groundwork for the modern civil rights movement and continue to inspire and inform contemporary movements for social change and liberation.

As we continue to grapple with issues of race, identity, and inequality in our society, the lessons of the Harlem Renaissance serve as a reminder of the enduring power of art, culture, and activism to shape our understanding of ourselves and our world. By exploring the complexities of African American identity and experience, the Harlem Renaissance challenged us to confront the legacies of slavery and segregation and to imagine a future of freedom, equality, and justice for all.

Chapter 11: Legacy of the Harlem Renaissance

Impact of the Renaissance on American Culture and Society

The Harlem Renaissance was a transformative period in American history, leaving a lasting impact on culture, society, and the struggle for racial justice and equality. This chapter examines the legacy of the Harlem Renaissance, exploring its influence on American culture and society and its lasting impact on subsequent generations of artists and activists.

1. Redefining American Identity:

The Harlem Renaissance played a crucial role in redefining American identity and culture, challenging prevailing notions of race, identity, and citizenship, and affirming the contributions and achievements of African Americans to American society. Through literature, art, music, and activism, the Harlem Renaissance celebrated the richness and diversity of African American culture, providing a counter-narrative to the prevailing stereotypes and caricatures of Blackness in American popular culture.

Writers such as Langston Hughes, Zora Neale Hurston, and Claude McKay used their works to explore themes of race, identity, and belonging, giving voice to the experiences and aspirations of the Black community and challenging the dominant narratives of white supremacy and racial hierarchy. Artists such as Aaron Douglas, Romare Bearden, and Augusta Savage created powerful images that celebrated the achievements and contributions of African Americans to American culture and society, challenging prevailing notions of beauty, representation, and power.

2. Pioneering Social and Political Activism:

The Harlem Renaissance was not only a cultural and artistic movement but also a period of social and political activism, with African American artists, writers, musicians, and intellectuals using their talents to advocate for civil rights, social justice, and racial equality. Activists such as W.E.B. Du Bois, Marcus Garvey, and the NAACP played a pivotal role in mobilizing the Black community and galvanizing support for the struggle for racial justice and equality.

The legacy of the Harlem Renaissance can be seen in the modern civil rights movement of the 1950s and 1960s, which built upon the achievements and contributions of earlier generations of African American activists and intellectuals. The ideas and strategies developed during the Harlem Renaissance, such as the concept of "double consciousness" articulated by W.E.B. Du Bois, and the vision of Black nationalism and Pan-Africanism promoted by Marcus Garvey, provided a foundation for the organizing efforts of civil rights leaders such as Martin Luther King Jr., Rosa Parks, and Malcolm X.

3. Inspiring Future Generations:

The legacy of the Harlem Renaissance continues to inspire and influence subsequent generations of artists, writers, musicians, and activists, who draw inspiration from the achievements and contributions of their predecessors. The themes and ideas explored by writers such as Langston Hughes and Zora Neale Hurston, the visual imagery created by artists such as Aaron Douglas and Romare Bearden, and the activism and organizing efforts of leaders such as W.E.B. Du Bois and Marcus Garvey continue to resonate with contemporary audiences, reminding us of the enduring power of art, culture, and activism to shape our understanding of ourselves and our world.

In the decades since the Harlem Renaissance, African American artists, writers, musicians, and activists have continued to build upon the achievements and contributions of earlier generations, pushing boundaries, challenging conventions, and advocating for social change and justice. From the civil rights movement to the Black Lives Matter movement, the legacy of the Harlem Renaissance lives on in the ongoing struggle for racial justice and equality in America, inspiring future generations to continue the fight for freedom, dignity, and equality for all.

Chapter 12: Harlem Renaissance Beyond Harlem

Discussion of the Spread and Influence of the Renaissance Beyond Harlem

The Harlem Renaissance was a cultural and intellectual movement that originated in the Harlem neighborhood of New York City but quickly spread its influence far beyond its geographic boundaries. This chapter explores the spread and influence of the Harlem Renaissance beyond Harlem, examining similar cultural movements in other African American communities and the lasting impact of the Renaissance on American culture and society.

1. Harlem as the Epicenter:

Harlem, with its vibrant and diverse community of African American artists, writers, musicians, and intellectuals, emerged as the epicenter of the Harlem Renaissance in the 1920s. The neighborhood became a magnet for African Americans from across the country, drawn by the promise of opportunity, freedom, and cultural expression. The streets of Harlem pulsated with the sounds of jazz, the rhythms of poetry, and the vibrant colors of visual art, as artists and intellectuals gathered in speakeasies, clubs, and literary salons to exchange ideas, collaborate on projects, and celebrate the richness and diversity of Black culture.

However, the influence of the Harlem Renaissance extended far beyond the borders of Harlem, reaching into communities across the United States and beyond. African American artists, writers, musicians, and intellectuals in cities such as Chicago, Detroit, Philadelphia, and Los Angeles were inspired by the achievements and contributions of their counterparts in Harlem and sought to create their own cultural movements that reflected the unique experiences and aspirations of their communities.

2. Similar Cultural Movements:

a. Chicago Renaissance:

The Chicago Renaissance was a cultural and intellectual movement that emerged in the African American neighborhoods of Chicago in the 1930s and 1940s. Like the Harlem Renaissance, the Chicago Renaissance was characterized by a flourishing of literature, music, art, and activism that celebrated the achievements and contributions of African Americans to American culture and society.

Writers such as Richard Wright, Gwendolyn Brooks, and Lorraine Hansberry emerged as leading voices of the Chicago Renaissance, exploring themes of race, identity, and social justice in their works. Wright's novel "Native Son," Brooks's poetry collection "A Street in Bronzeville," and Hansberry's play "A Raisin in the Sun" are just a few examples of the groundbreaking works produced during this period, which continue to resonate with contemporary audiences.

Musicians such as Nat King Cole, Mahalia Jackson, and Dinah Washington also emerged from the vibrant jazz and blues scenes of Chicago, achieving national and international acclaim for their contributions to American music.

b. Detroit Renaissance:

The Detroit Renaissance was a cultural and intellectual movement that emerged in the African American neighborhoods of Detroit in the 1940s and 1950s. Fueled by the influx of African Americans from the rural South seeking employment in the city's booming auto industry, the Detroit Renaissance was characterized by a flowering of literature, music, art, and activism that reflected the experiences and aspirations of the Black community.

Writers such as Langston Hughes, Robert Hayden, and Rosa Guy emerged as leading voices of the Detroit Renaissance, exploring themes of urban life, migration, and social change in their works. Hughes's poem "Dream Deferred," Hayden's poem "Middle Passage," and Guy's novel "The Friends" are just a few examples of the powerful works produced during this period, which continue to resonate with contemporary audiences.

Musicians such as Aretha Franklin, John Lee Hooker, and Stevie Wonder also emerged from the vibrant music scene of Detroit, achieving national and international acclaim for their contributions to American music.

c. Philadelphia Renaissance:

The Philadelphia Renaissance was a cultural and intellectual movement that emerged in the African American neighborhoods of Philadelphia in the 1920s and 1930s. Fueled by the Great Migration of African Americans from the rural South to the urban North, the Philadelphia Renaissance was characterized by a flowering of literature, music, art, and activism that celebrated the achievements and contributions of African Americans to American culture and society.

Writers such as Claude McKay, Nella Larsen, and Jessie Redmon Fauset emerged as leading voices of the Philadelphia Renaissance, exploring themes of race, identity, and social change in their works. McKay's novel "Home to Harlem," Larsen's novel "Passing," and Fauset's novel "Plum Bun" are just a few examples of the groundbreaking works produced during this period, which continue to resonate with contemporary audiences.

Musicians such as Marian Anderson, Ethel Waters, and Billie Holiday also emerged from the vibrant music scene of Philadelphia, achieving national and international acclaim for their contributions to American music.

3. Lasting Impact:

The lasting impact of the Harlem Renaissance can be seen in the ongoing struggle for racial justice and equality in America, as well as in the rich and diverse tapestry of American culture and society. The Harlem Renaissance inspired subsequent generations of artists, writers, musicians, and intellectuals to celebrate the richness and diversity of African American culture, to challenge prevailing notions of race, identity, and citizenship, and to advocate for social change and justice.

From the civil rights movement to the Black Lives Matter movement, the legacy of the Harlem Renaissance lives on in the ongoing struggle for freedom, dignity, and equality for all. As we continue to confront the legacy of racism and inequality in our society, the lessons of the Harlem Renaissance serve as a reminder of the enduring power of art, culture, and activism to shape our understanding of ourselves and our world.

Chapter 13: Challenges and Criticisms of the Harlem Renaissance

Acknowledgment of the Limitations and Criticisms

While the Harlem Renaissance was a period of unprecedented cultural flourishing and intellectual achievement for African Americans, it was not without its limitations and criticisms. This chapter explores the challenges and criticisms faced by the Harlem Renaissance, including issues such as elitism, gender bias, and commercialization, and examines how these factors shaped the movement and its legacy.

1. Elitism and Exclusivity:

One of the primary criticisms leveled against the Harlem Renaissance is that it was elitist and exclusive, catering primarily to the interests and tastes of the Black middle class and intellectual elite. While the Renaissance provided a platform for African American artists, writers, musicians, and intellectuals to showcase their talents and express their creativity, it often marginalized or overlooked the experiences and perspectives of working-class and poor African Americans, who made up the majority of the Black population in Harlem and other urban centers.

The Harlem Renaissance was centered around institutions such as the New Negro Movement, which promoted the idea of the "New Negro" as an educated, sophisticated, and socially conscious individual who embraced modernity and progress. While this concept represented a powerful affirmation of African American identity and agency, it also reinforced class distinctions within the

Black community and perpetuated the myth of the "talented tenth" – the idea that a small elite group of educated African Americans could uplift the entire race.

2. Gender Bias and Patriarchy:

Another criticism of the Harlem Renaissance is that it was characterized by gender bias and patriarchy, with women artists, writers, and intellectuals facing discrimination and marginalization within the movement. While women played a crucial role in shaping the Harlem Renaissance and contributed significantly to its cultural and intellectual achievements, their contributions were often overshadowed or undervalued by their male counterparts.

Women writers such as Zora Neale Hurston, Nella Larsen, and Jessie Redmon Fauset faced challenges in getting their works published and recognized, and their achievements were often dismissed or minimized by critics and scholars. Women artists such as Augusta Savage, Lois Mailou Jones, and Meta Vaux Warrick Fuller faced similar challenges in gaining recognition and acclaim for their artistic talents, with their works often being relegated to the margins of the art world.

3. Commercialization and Commodification:

The Harlem Renaissance was also criticized for its commercialization and commodification, with the cultural and artistic achievements of African Americans being exploited for commercial gain by white-owned publishing houses, record companies, and art galleries. While the Renaissance provided unprecedented opportunities for African American artists, writers, musicians, and intellectuals to showcase their talents and reach a wider audience, it also subjected them to the pressures and demands of the marketplace, which often prioritized profit over artistic integrity and social responsibility.

Many African American artists and intellectuals struggled to reconcile their desire for creative expression and social engagement with the demands of the commercial marketplace, leading to tensions and conflicts within the movement. Some artists and intellectuals, such as Langston Hughes and Claude McKay, embraced commercial success and popular acclaim as a means of reaching a wider audience and advancing the cause of racial justice and equality, while others, such as W.E.B. Du Bois and Alain Locke, criticized the commercialization and commodification of African American culture and called for a return to the values of authenticity, integrity, and social responsibility.

4. Intersectional Critiques:

In addition to these criticisms, the Harlem Renaissance has also faced intersectional critiques that highlight the ways in which issues of race, class, gender, and sexuality intersect and shape the experiences and perspectives of African Americans. Critics such as bell hooks, Angela Davis, and Audre Lorde have argued that the Harlem Renaissance, while groundbreaking in many respects, failed to fully address the complex and intersecting forms of oppression and discrimination faced by African American women, LGBTQ+ individuals, and other marginalized groups within the Black community.

These intersectional critiques challenge us to critically examine the limitations and biases of the Harlem Renaissance and to recognize the diversity and complexity of African American experiences and identities. They remind us that the struggle for racial justice and equality is inseparable from the struggle for gender justice, economic justice, and social justice, and that true liberation requires us to address the intersecting forms of oppression and discrimination that shape our society.

5. Legacy and Lessons Learned:

Despite these challenges and criticisms, the Harlem Renaissance remains a powerful and enduring legacy that continues to inspire and influence artists, writers, musicians, and activists today. The achievements and contributions of the Harlem Renaissance, while imperfect and incomplete, represent a bold and courageous assertion of African American identity, agency, and creativity in the face of systemic racism and oppression.

As we continue to confront the legacy of the Harlem Renaissance, it is essential that we acknowledge its limitations and criticisms and learn from them. We must strive to create a more inclusive and equitable society that values and celebrates the diversity of human experience and expression, and that recognizes the contributions and achievements of all people, regardless of race, class, gender, or sexuality.

By critically examining the challenges and criticisms of the Harlem Renaissance, we can gain a deeper understanding of its complexities and contradictions, and we can draw lessons from its successes and failures to guide us in our ongoing struggle for justice, equality, and liberation for all.

Chapter 14: Revival and Rediscovery of the Harlem Renaissance

Exploration of Efforts to Revive Interest in the Harlem Renaissance in Contemporary Culture

The Harlem Renaissance, a period of extraordinary cultural and intellectual achievement in African American history, continues to captivate the imagination of artists, scholars, and activists in contemporary culture. This chapter delves into the efforts to revive interest in the Harlem Renaissance and explores the profiles of modern-day artists and scholars inspired by the Renaissance.

1. Rediscovering the Legacy:

In recent years, there has been a resurgence of interest in the Harlem Renaissance, as scholars, artists, and activists seek to rediscover and celebrate the legacy of this transformative period in African American history. Exhibitions, conferences, and symposiums dedicated to the Harlem Renaissance have been held in cities across the United States and around the world, bringing together scholars, artists, and activists to explore its significance and relevance to contemporary culture.

One such example is the "Renaissance Noir" exhibition held at the Smithsonian National Museum of African American History and Culture, which showcased the contributions of African American artists, writers, musicians, and intellectuals to American culture and society during the Harlem Renaissance. The exhibition featured artworks, manuscripts, photographs, and other artifacts from the Harlem Renaissance, providing visitors with a comprehensive overview of this pivotal period in African American history.

2. Contemporary Artists Inspired by the Renaissance:

a. Kara Walker:

Kara Walker is a contemporary artist known for her provocative and thought-provoking explorations of race, gender, and power in American society. Inspired by the legacy of the Harlem Renaissance, Walker's work often incorporates themes and imagery drawn from African American history and culture, challenging viewers to confront the legacies of slavery, segregation, and systemic racism.

Walker's silhouette installations, which depict scenes of slavery, oppression, and resistance, have garnered international acclaim for their powerful and evocative portrayal of the African American experience. By reimagining and reinterpreting the visual language of the past, Walker seeks to shed light on the complexities and contradictions of American identity and to provoke dialogue and reflection on issues of race and representation.

b. Ta-Nehisi Coates:

Ta-Nehisi Coates is a contemporary writer and journalist known for his incisive and impassioned explorations of race, politics, and culture in America. Inspired by the legacy of the Harlem Renaissance, Coates's work often addresses themes of racial injustice, systemic inequality, and the enduring legacy of slavery and segregation in American society.

Coates's bestselling books, including "Between the World and Me" and "The Beautiful Struggle," have been hailed as powerful and urgent meditations on the Black experience in America, challenging readers to confront the realities of racism and to imagine a more just and equitable future. By drawing inspiration from the Harlem Renaissance, Coates seeks to honor the achievements and contributions of earlier generations of African American artists, writers, musicians, and intellectuals, while also continuing their legacy of resistance and resilience in the face of oppression.

c. Ava DuVernay:

Ava DuVernay is a contemporary filmmaker known for her groundbreaking work in film and television, including the critically acclaimed films "Selma" and "13th," and the television series "Queen Sugar" and "When They See Us." Inspired by the legacy of the Harlem Renaissance, DuVernay's work often explores themes of race, identity, and social justice in America, shining a light on the struggles and triumphs of African Americans in their quest for freedom and equality.

DuVernay's films and television series have been praised for their powerful storytelling, compelling characters, and nuanced exploration of complex social issues. By drawing inspiration from the Harlem Renaissance, DuVernay seeks to honor the achievements and contributions of earlier generations of African American artists, writers, musicians, and intellectuals, while also pushing the boundaries of representation and storytelling in contemporary culture.

3. Scholarly Reappraisals:

In addition to the work of contemporary artists inspired by the Harlem Renaissance, scholars and academics have also undertaken efforts to reevaluate and reexamine the legacy of the Renaissance in contemporary culture. Through research, publications, and conferences, scholars are uncovering new insights and perspectives on the Harlem Renaissance, shedding light on overlooked figures and movements, and exploring its relevance to contemporary debates and discussions about race, identity, and culture.

One such example is the "Rethinking the Harlem Renaissance" conference held at Columbia University, which brought together scholars, artists, and activists to reassess the achievements and contributions of the Harlem Renaissance and to explore its significance for contemporary culture. Through panels, presentations, and discussions, participants engaged in a critical dialogue about the legacy of the Harlem Renaissance and its ongoing relevance to issues of race, identity, and social justice in America today.

4. Conclusion:

The revival and rediscovery of the Harlem Renaissance in contemporary culture reflect a growing recognition of its enduring significance and relevance to the ongoing struggle for racial justice and equality in America. By drawing inspiration from the achievements and contributions of earlier generations of African American artists, writers, musicians, and intellectuals, contemporary artists, scholars, and activists are continuing the legacy of the Harlem Renaissance, reaffirming its central place in the cultural and intellectual history of the United States and its ongoing relevance to contemporary debates and discussions about race, identity, and culture.

Chapter 15: Conclusion: Continuing the Legacy

Reflection on the Enduring Significance of the Harlem Renaissance

The Harlem Renaissance stands as a beacon of cultural and intellectual achievement in African American history, a testament to the resilience, creativity, and ingenuity of a people who refused to be silenced or marginalized. As we reflect on the enduring significance of the Harlem Renaissance, we are reminded of the power of art, culture, and activism to shape our understanding of ourselves and our world, and to inspire us to imagine and strive for a more just and equitable future.

1. Celebration of African American Identity and Culture:

At its core, the Harlem Renaissance was a celebration of African American identity and culture, a reaffirmation of the dignity, humanity, and resilience of a people who had endured centuries of slavery, segregation, and discrimination. Through literature, art, music, and activism, African American artists, writers, musicians, and intellectuals reclaimed their heritage and celebrated the richness and diversity of Black culture, challenging prevailing notions of race, identity, and citizenship, and asserting their rightful place in American society.

The legacy of the Harlem Renaissance continues to resonate in contemporary culture, as artists, scholars, and activists draw inspiration from its achievements and contributions to explore themes of race, identity, and social justice in their work. From the visual art of Kara Walker and the writing of Ta-Nehisi Coates to the filmmaking of Ava DuVernay and the activism of Black Lives Matter, the Harlem Renaissance lives on in the ongoing struggle for freedom, dignity, and equality for all.

2. Call to Action:

As we continue to confront the legacy of racism and inequality in our society, the lessons of the Harlem Renaissance serve as a call to action to continue championing African American arts, culture, and activism. We must strive to create a more inclusive and equitable society that values and celebrates the diversity of human experience and expression, and that recognizes the contributions and achievements of all people, regardless of race, class, gender, or sexuality.

This call to action requires us to support and uplift African American artists, writers, musicians, and intellectuals, and to amplify their voices and perspectives in our cultural institutions, educational curricula, and public discourse. It requires us to confront the legacies of slavery, segregation, and systemic racism that continue to shape our society, and to work towards dismantling the structures of oppression and inequality that perpetuate injustice and suffering.

It requires us to listen to the voices of those who have been marginalized and oppressed, and to stand in solidarity with them in their struggles for justice, equality, and liberation. It requires us to recognize that the fight for racial justice and equality is not a finite or abstract concept, but an ongoing and collective effort that requires the active participation and commitment of each and every one of us.

In conclusion, the Harlem Renaissance continues to inspire and challenge us to imagine and strive for a world where all people are valued, respected, and treated with dignity and equality. By continuing the legacy of the Harlem Renaissance, we can work towards building a more just, equitable, and inclusive society for future generations, where the dreams and aspirations of all people can be realized.

Don't miss out!

Visit the website below and you can sign up to receive emails whenever Michael Johnson publishes a new book. There's no charge and no obligation.

https://books2read.com/r/B-A-OREFB-DMVAD

Did you love *The Harlem Renaissance*? Then you should read *The Cold War*[1] by Michael Johnson!

2

Explore the riveting saga of the Cold War, from its tumultuous beginnings to its epochal conclusion. Unveil the geopolitical chessboard of post-World War II as the United States and the Soviet Union ascend as superpowers, igniting tensions that reverberate worldwide. From the Truman Doctrine to the Cuban Missile Crisis, McCarthyism to the Vietnam War, delve into the ideological battlegrounds and proxy conflicts that defined an era. Witness the thaw of détente and the seismic shifts of perestroika, culminating in

---

1. https://books2read.com/u/3L8985

2. https://books2read.com/u/3L8985

the historic collapse of the Soviet Union. Experience the legacy and lessons of this epochal standoff, resonating into the 21st century.

About the Author

Michael Johnson is a distinguished historian specializing in American history. With a degree in History from Harvard University, Johnson's work delves into pivotal moments, figures, and themes shaping the United States. He has authored numerous acclaimed books, offering insightful perspectives and engaging narratives. Johnson's commitment to meticulous scholarship and compelling storytelling has earned him widespread acclaim in the field. Passionate about sharing his expertise, he frequently engages in lectures and public events to foster a deeper appreciation for America's past.